WEIRD ANIMALS DICTIONARY

An **A** to **Z** of the world's most bizarre creatures

Information icons

Throughout this dictionary, there are special icons next to each entry. These give you more information about each creature.

Globes

These show you where each creature can be found in the world. Small red dots on the globes clearly show the locations.

Size comparison pictures

Next to each entry you will see a black symbol (e.g. eye, hand) next to a red icon of the creature listed. These show you the size of each animal in real life compared to the size of a human.

The first symbol is a magnifying glass, which will appear next to the creatures that are difficult to see without a microscope.

2.5 cm

The second symbol is a human eye, which measure about 2.5 cm (1 in) across. Many creatures are smaller than this, so this symbol will help you imagine their size.

18 cm

The third symbol is a human adult's hand, which measures about 18 cm (7 in) from the wrist to the tip of the longest finger. Some creatures are smaller than this, so this symbol will help you to comparetheir length to a hand.

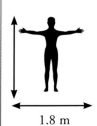

1.8 m

The forth symbol is an adult human. The height of the human is about 1.8 metres (6 ft). With arms outstretched, the arm span measures about 1.8 metres (6 ft). This symbol will help you to compare the height or length of a creature to a human.

1.8 m

The fifth symbol is an adult diver. The length of a diver measures about 1.8 metres (6 ft). This symbol will help you to imagine the length of some creatures

© 2009 Alligator Books Ltd
Cupcake is an imprint of Alligator Books Ltd
Gadd House, Arcadia Avenue
London N3 2JU

Printed in China. 10893

WEIRD ANIMALS DICTIONARY

An **A** to **Z** of the world's most bizarre creatures

cupcake

What is wierd?

What is it that makes one animal seem weird while others seem quite ordinary? It all depends on the point of view. Extracting a dangerous, explosive and corrosive gas from the atmosphere might seem like a weird thing to do, but that is what happens when most animals breathe oxygen – and that includes those weirdly smart animals known as human beings.

Water bear

Weird animals?

From a human viewpoint, a weird animal is one that either looks or behaves in a way that is very different from human beings. However, humans are just one species among an estimated ten million or so that are currently living on this planet.

Basilisk lizard

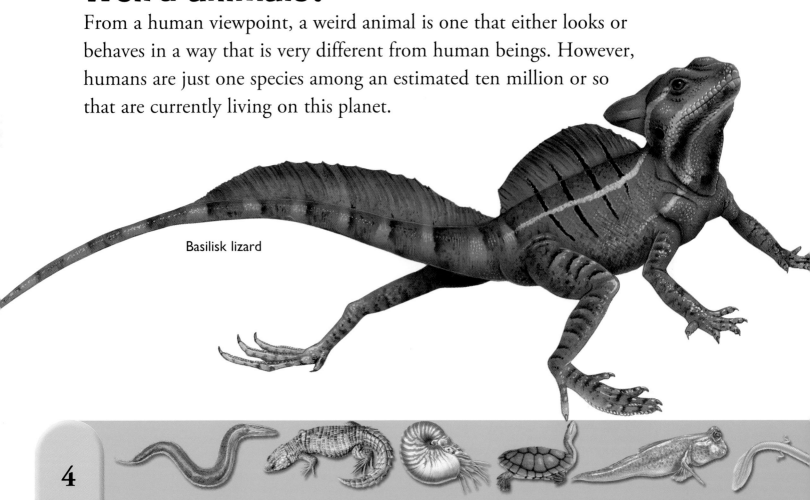

Most of the other species are impossibly weird by comparison with humans – they may be cold-blooded, boneless, brainless, limbless or even stranger than that.

Amazing animals

Any scientist will tell you that life is a strange, weird and wonderful thing. It is impossible to study biology (science of living things), zoology (science of animals) or botany (science of plants) without a sense of amazement, wonder and delight. Some of our fellow creatures are just so bizarre that they make you want to clap your hands and shout out loud, 'Wow! Look at this! It is really weird!'

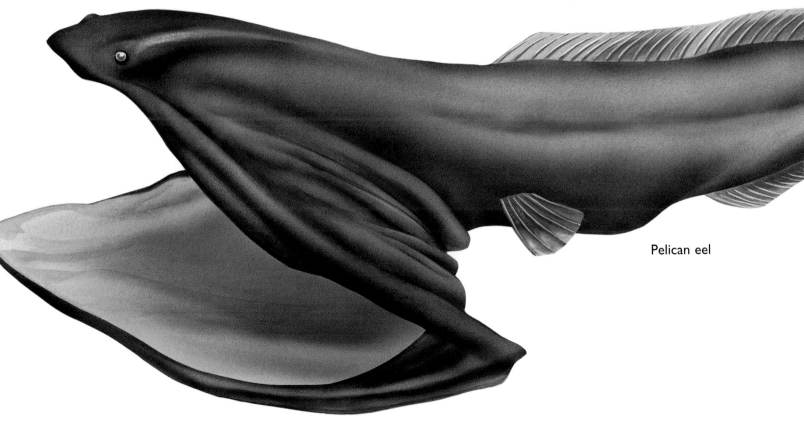

Flying lemur

Pelican eel

Animal groups

We may think of animals as having four legs, a head and a tail, that birds have wings, and that fish live in the sea, but animal life is a lot more complicated and many creatures look quite different. In addition to the easily recognisable animal groups – mammals, birds, reptiles, amphibians and fish – all of which are vertebrates (they have an internal skeleton), there are many others that are invertebrates (they lack an internal skeleton). All come in different shapes, sizes and colours.

Holothurian

Fish and whales

Fish are cold-blooded and live in the sea, while most mammals are warm-blooded, walk on land, and are covered with fur to keep them warm. Yet the largest animals in the sea are gigantic, hairless mammals – whales. This may seem weird, but despite their many differences, fish and whales are quite similar – especially when compared to other sea animals such as brittle stars, horseshoe crabs and cuttlefish. This is just one example of our 'weird' animal world.

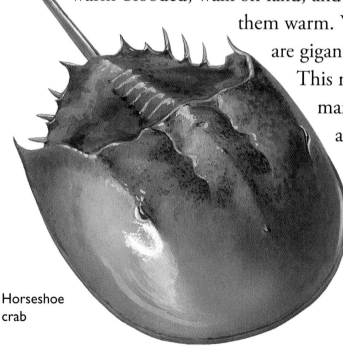

Horseshoe crab

Microscopic animals

An animal is something that eats, breathes, moves and reproduces; and there are a great many animals that are too small to see with the unaided eye. When viewed through a microscope, these tiny animals reveal a staggering variety of body shapes and behaviour. Many of these microscopic animals live in water, and a single drop may contain more than a dozen different species. When viewed under proper conditions, watching the feeding behaviour of a paramecium is every bit as exciting as watching a lion or a shark hunting for prey.

Paramecium

Amoeba

Paddlefish

7

Aa

Max length: 1.6 m (5¼ ft)

Aardvark

Also known as the ant bear, the aardvark is one of a kind. This unusual mammal is found in Central and southern Africa and has no close relatives. It has a pig-like snout and strong teeth in its jaws, but it hardly ever uses its teeth to bite or chew food. It prefers to gather up ants and termites with its long tongue and swallow them whole.

Fact
The aardvark is one of the best diggers in the animal world. It uses its powerful claws to make burrows that are more than 10 metres (33 ft) in length.

Max length: 24 cm (9½ in)

Ajolte

The ajolte is sometimes misleadingly called a mole lizard. It is a strange reptile that looks like a snake or a legless lizard, but is in fact neither. The ajolte is found in Mexico and belongs to a group of reptiles called amphisbaenas. It has a pair of short, but very strong forelegs that are used for digging.

Amoeba

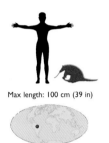

Max length: 5 mm (⅕ in)

worldwide

An amoeba is generally microscopic and is just about the most simple animal there is. It is a single cell with no brain, no senses and no definite shape. It is a tiny blob of living jelly that can do little else but move and eat. It moves by slowly 'flowing' across a surface – reaching out and then catching up with itself. An amoeba eats by engulfing a particle of food inside its body where it is slowly absorbed.

Armadillo

Max length: 100 cm (39 in)

The armadillo is perhaps the most unusual-looking mammal. Although its skin has a few hairs like other mammals, the armadillo also has unique overlapping plates of armour made of horn and bone. The South American giant armadillo is strong enough to dig through a concrete road.

Bb

Bactrian camel

Max length: 3 m (10 ft)

With two humps and a distinctive shaggy coat, the Bactrian camel is the only wild camel. The one-humped camel (also known as a dromedary) is a domesticated species. Some Bactrian camels have also been domesticated and are still used for transport in central Asia. However, there are still some completely wild camels living in the most remote parts of the cold, central Asian deserts.

Barnacle

Max length: 10 cm (4 in)

worldwide

The barnacle is a familiar sight along rocky shorelines. Most people think that it is a type of mollusc like oysters, clams and mussels. In fact, the barnacle belongs to the same group as crabs and shrimps – the crustaceans. Unlike its relatives, which swim and walk along the seabed, the barnacle has a fixed existence and uses its legs to catch food particles in the water.

Max length: 76 cm (30 in)

Basilisk lizard

It does not have wings or breathe fire, but the basilisk is
fairly close to many people's ideas of what a dragon might
look like. It has a long, flexible body and tail, slender limbs with sharp
claws and a large head with powerful jaws. Fortunately, the real-life
basilisk lizard, which lives in Central America, is much smaller than its
fictional look-alike – and is only frightening to small prey such as beetles
and cockroaches.

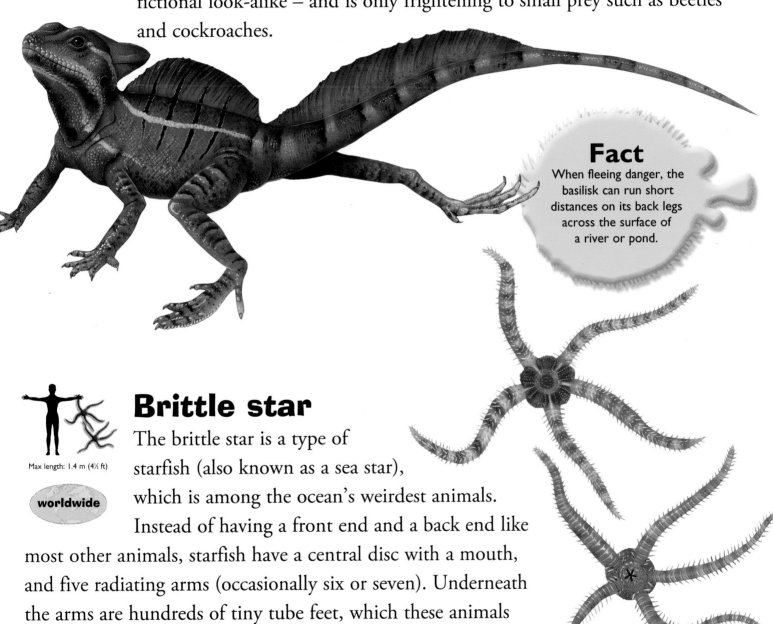

Fact
When fleeing danger, the
basilisk can run short
distances on its back legs
across the surface of
a river or pond.

Max length: 1.4 m (4½ ft)

worldwide

Brittle star

The brittle star is a type of
starfish (also known as a sea star),
which is among the ocean's weirdest animals.
Instead of having a front end and a back end like
most other animals, starfish have a central disc with a mouth,
and five radiating arms (occasionally six or seven). Underneath
the arms are hundreds of tiny tube feet, which these animals
use to walk over the seabed.

Cc

Max length: 1.5 m (5 ft)

Caecilian

The caecilian is a peculiar worm-shaped animal that lives almost entirely underground in tunnels beneath lake beds. It is often mistaken for a snake or an eel, but it is neither fish nor reptile. Caecilians are actually a group of legless amphibians that are related to frogs and salamanders.

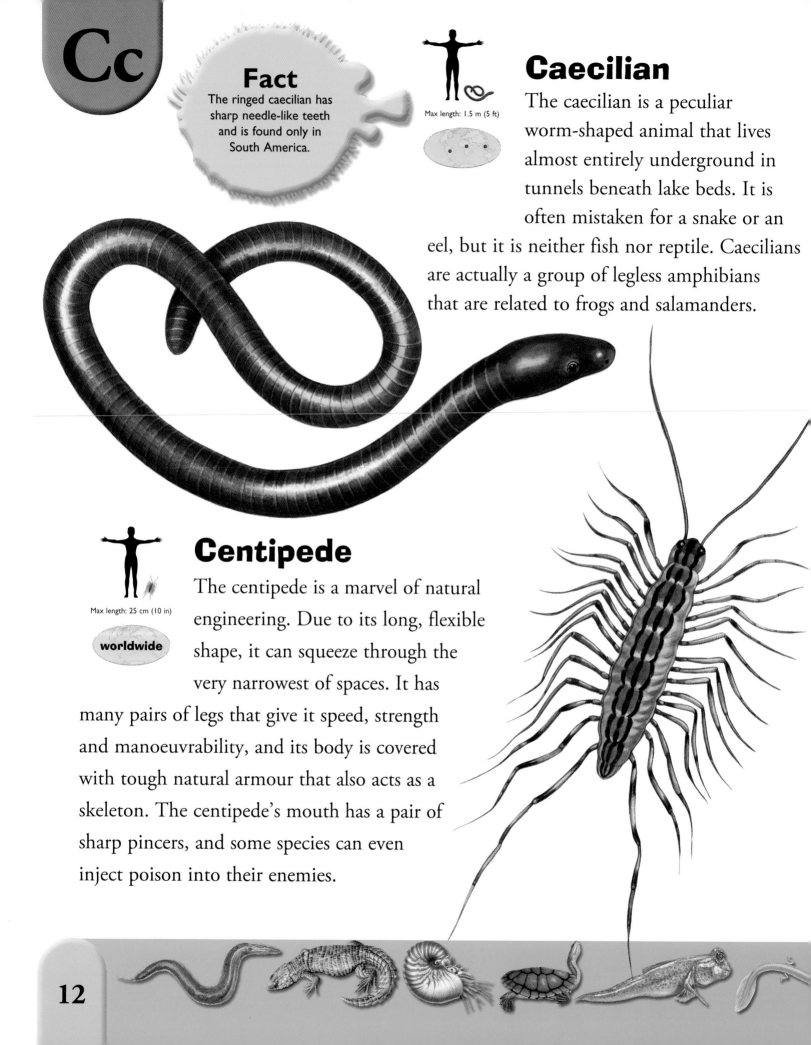

Max length: 25 cm (10 in)

worldwide

Centipede

The centipede is a marvel of natural engineering. Due to its long, flexible shape, it can squeeze through the very narrowest of spaces. It has many pairs of legs that give it speed, strength and manoeuvrability, and its body is covered with tough natural armour that also acts as a skeleton. The centipede's mouth has a pair of sharp pincers, and some species can even inject poison into their enemies.

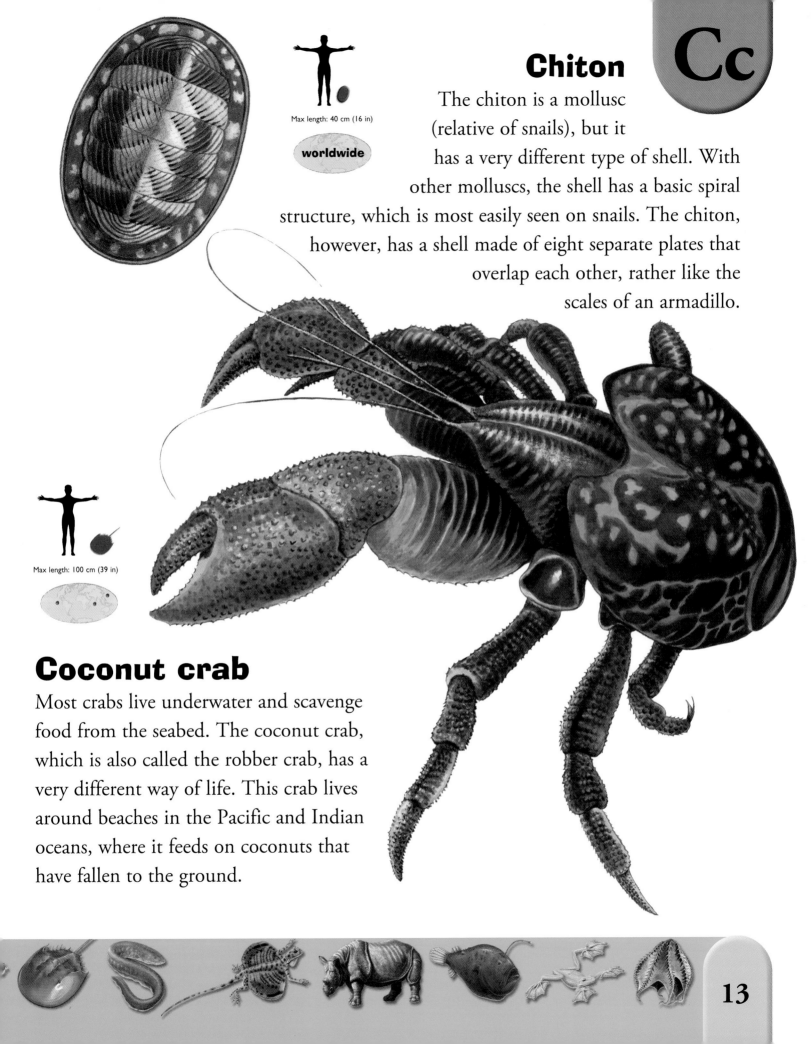

Chiton

Max length: 40 cm (16 in)

worldwide

The chiton is a mollusc (relative of snails), but it has a very different type of shell. With other molluscs, the shell has a basic spiral structure, which is most easily seen on snails. The chiton, however, has a shell made of eight separate plates that overlap each other, rather like the scales of an armadillo.

Max length: 100 cm (39 in)

Coconut crab

Most crabs live underwater and scavenge food from the seabed. The coconut crab, which is also called the robber crab, has a very different way of life. This crab lives around beaches in the Pacific and Indian oceans, where it feeds on coconuts that have fallen to the ground.

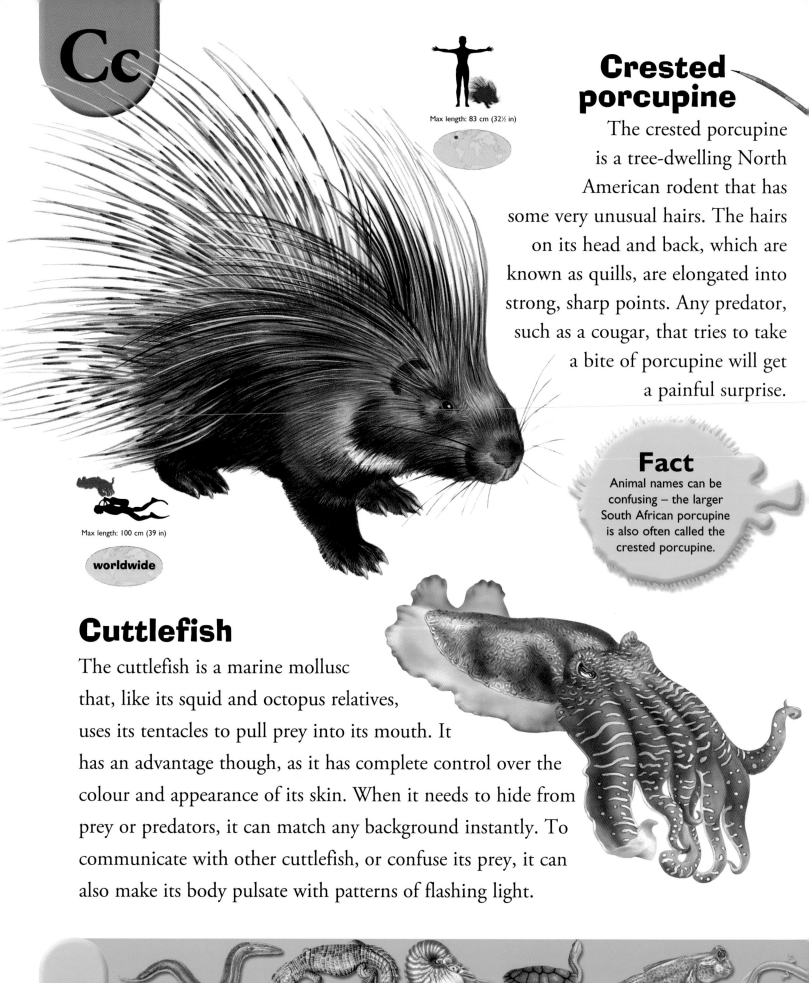

Max length: 83 cm (32½ in)

Crested porcupine

The crested porcupine is a tree-dwelling North American rodent that has some very unusual hairs. The hairs on its head and back, which are known as quills, are elongated into strong, sharp points. Any predator, such as a cougar, that tries to take a bite of porcupine will get a painful surprise.

Fact

Animal names can be confusing – the larger South African porcupine is also often called the crested porcupine.

Max length: 100 cm (39 in)

worldwide

Cuttlefish

The cuttlefish is a marine mollusc that, like its squid and octopus relatives, uses its tentacles to pull prey into its mouth. It has an advantage though, as it has complete control over the colour and appearance of its skin. When it needs to hide from prey or predators, it can match any background instantly. To communicate with other cuttlefish, or confuse its prey, it can also make its body pulsate with patterns of flashing light.

Dd

Max length: 11 cm (4⅓ in)

Deadleaf butterfly

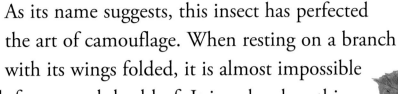

As its name suggests, this insect has perfected the art of camouflage. When resting on a branch with its wings folded, it is almost impossible to distinguish from a real dead leaf. It is only when this butterfly moves that its perfect disguise is spoiled.

Max length: 20 cm (8 in)

Draco

The draco (the name means dragon) is also know as the flying lizard, although this is slightly misleading. This reptile does not actually fly, but uses flaps of skin along the sides of its body to glide from branch to branch through the tropical forests of Indonesia.

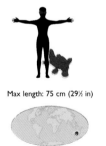

Max length: 75 cm (29½ in)

Duck-billed platypus

The platypus, which lives in Australian rivers, is undoubtedly the weirdest mammal in the world. Its unique duckbill is used for detecting the electrical energy of prey such as freshwater shrimp. In addition, the platypus is one of only three mammals that lay eggs.

Ee

Max length: 76 cm (2½ ft)

Echidna

The long-nosed echidna is another very weird mammal Together with its close relatives, the spiny echidna and the platypus, it is one of the monotremes (egg-laying mammals). The echidna is a forest animal that hunts at night for termites and ants. It is protected from predators by hundreds of sharp spines, which are just visible through its thick fur.

Fact
The female echidna digs deep burrows to protect its eggs. After hatching, it carries its young in a pouch.

Max length: 2.5 m (8 ft)

Electric eel

This large fish from the rivers of South America has poor eyesight and uses weak pulses of electricity to detect fish and other prey in murky water. Special muscles along the eel's body produce this electricity. When threatened, it can deliver a very strong pulse of electricity (up to 600 volts), which is enough to stun or kill a human being.

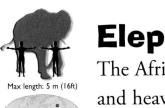

Max length: 5 m (16ft)

Elephant

The African elephant is the biggest and heaviest land animal. A fully-grown male is more than 4 metres (13 ft) tall and weighs up to 7 tonnes (7½ tons). The African elephant, along with its smaller Indian cousin, is unique in having a long, flexible trunk for a nose. As well as being a highly-efficient sense organ, this weird nose is also used to gather up mouthfuls of grass and to pluck fruit from trees.

Max length: 1.2 m (4 ft)

Elephant fish

The elephant fish belongs to a group known as chimaeras, which are related to sharks and rays. It is also known as the plough-nose chimaera because of its distinctive snout. The elephant fish normally stays in deep water and only occasionally swims close to the surface.

Ff

Max length: 40 cm (15¾ in)

worldwide

Feather star

The feather star is a weird relative of the starfish. When young, the feather star is attached to rocks by a long stem. It gathers food with its feathery arms and looks just like an underwater plant. As an adult, it crawls about the seabed using a series of short arms and collects food with its long arms.

Fact

The feather star behaves in a similar manner to the hydra when young, but they are very different animals.

Max length: 2 m (6½ ft)

worldwide

Flatfish

A flatfish has the same shape as other fish when it is young. By the time it is 40 days old, its body starts to flatten out and one eye gradually moves across to the other side of its head – the upper side. When it is an adult, the fish is completely flat and swims on one side of its body.

Max length: 4 cm (1½ in)

Flower mantis

The flower mantis is one of the most beautiful, and one of the most perfectly camouflaged, of all animals. This insect predator has developed a shape and colour that makes it look like a tropical flower. The mantis sits on a real flower and waits patiently for its prey. When an insect comes to investigate the flower, the mantis grabs the insect.

Fact

The front-leg strike of the mantis is one of the fastest movements in the animal kingdom.

Max length: 15 cm (6 in)

Flowerpot snake

The flowerpot snake is a small blind snake that is often found in the most unusual places. Originally from southern Asia, where it is known as the Brahminy blindsnake, it has been transported all over the world inside shipments of houseplants.

Ff

Max length: 40 cm (15¾ in)

Flying lemur

The flying lemur, which is also known as a colugo, has a very misleading name. Firstly, this animal can glide up to 100 metres (330 ft) between trees, but it cannot fly – bats are the only mammals that can actually fly. Secondly, it is not a lemur, which is a distant relative of monkeys, nor is it closely related to the similar looking flying squirrel. The two species of flying lemur are in fact in a class of their own.

Frilled lizard

Max length: 70 cm (2¼ ft)

The frilled lizard of Australia and New Guinea has one of the most spectacular defences of any animal on Earth. This medium-sized reptile has a frill of skin that normally hangs around its neck and shoulders. When threatened by a bird of prey, the lizard raises its frill, which makes its head look about five times bigger. The frilled lizard adds to the effect by opening its mouth wide and hissing.

Max length: 5 mm (⅕ in)

worldwide

Fungus gnat

The fungus gnat is a tiny flying insect, which feeds on fungi.

The larvae of one species from New Zealand, however, are carnivorous and they eat other insects. To catch their prey the larvae spin sticky glowing threads that are coated with poison. Attracted by the light, the prey is trapped, killed and is then eaten.

Ff
Gg

Fact
The larvae of the New Zealand fungus gnat are sometimes called glowworms, even though the larvae do not actually produce light.

Max height: 1.5 m (5 ft)

Giant panda

World famous as a symbol of endangered species, the giant panda is also quite a weird animal. The panda is the only animal apart from monkeys and apes that has 'thumbs' on its front paws. The panda's thumb is not a true, flexible thumb. It is a bony growth that helps the panda gather handfuls of bamboo, which is the only food that this animal will eat.

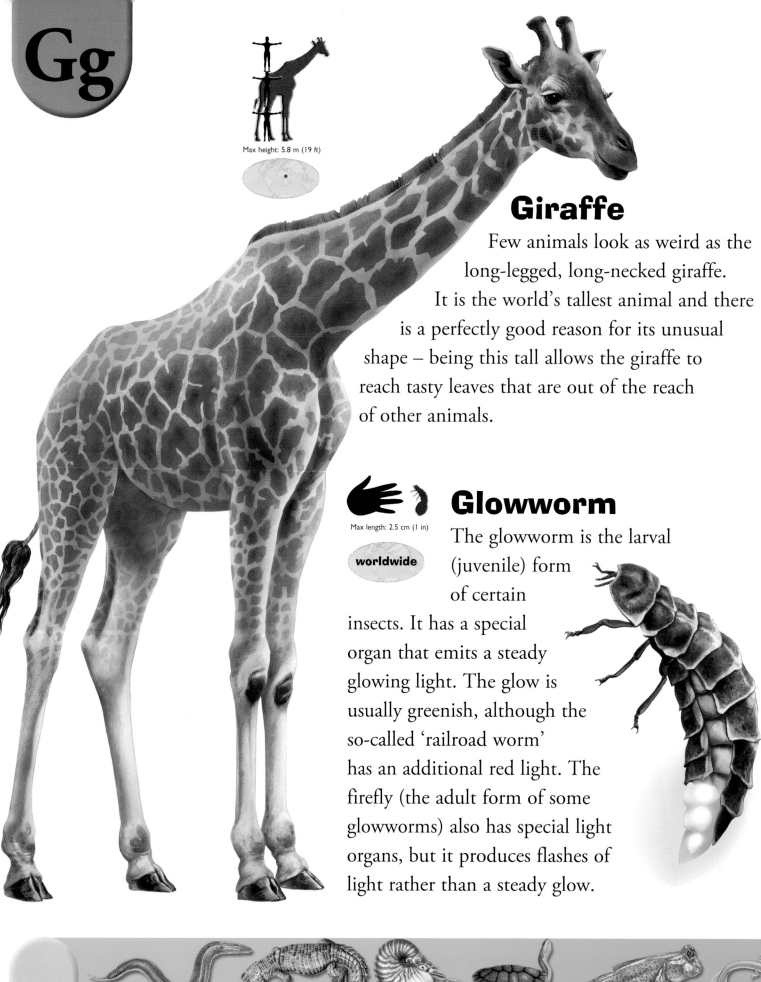

Gg

Max height: 5.8 m (19 ft)

Giraffe

Few animals look as weird as the long-legged, long-necked giraffe. It is the world's tallest animal and there is a perfectly good reason for its unusual shape – being this tall allows the giraffe to reach tasty leaves that are out of the reach of other animals.

Glowworm

Max length: 2.5 cm (1 in)

worldwide

The glowworm is the larval (juvenile) form of certain insects. It has a special organ that emits a steady glowing light. The glow is usually greenish, although the so-called 'railroad worm' has an additional red light. The firefly (the adult form of some glowworms) also has special light organs, but it produces flashes of light rather than a steady glow.

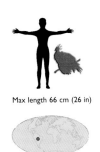

Hoatzin

Max length 66 cm (26 in)

This brightly-coloured South American bird has some very weird claws. All birds have claws (or talons) at the ends of their toes. The hoatzin, however, also has claws on its wings. At the elbow joint of each wing is a single curved claw. The hoatzin, which lives in swamps and flooded forests, uses these wing claws to help it climb out of the water.

Max length: 100 cm (39 in)

worldwide

Holothurian

A holothurian is the scientific name for a sea cucumber – a boneless sea animal that looks a bit like a giant caterpillar. Sea cucumbers are related to starfish and are found on seabeds in all but the coldest parts of the world. It has a unique defence system – if threatened, a sea cucumber can squirt sticky poisonous threads from its rear end to entangle its attacker.

Hh

Max length: 10 mm (½ in)

Honeypot ant

The honeypot ant has a unique natural storage system – its own body. This ant collects nectar and pollen from flowers and turns it into honey. Instead of storing the honey in a wax comb like bees, some of the ants themselves are used as storage containers. Filled with honey from other ants, they cling to the ceilings of the ants' nest until their honey is needed.

Max length: 36 cm (14 in)

Horned chameleon

The chameleon not only looks weird, but it also behaves very strangely. This slow-moving reptile can change colour to blend in with its background. It can also swivel each of its eyes, so that they can look in two directions at once. But even more weird is the chameleon's tongue, which is almost as long as its body and which it can shoot out with incredible speed to catch an insect on the sticky tip.

Horseshoe crab

Max length: 60 cm (24 in)

This very unusual sea creature is more closely related to spiders than to true crabs and is known as a 'living fossil'. The weird appearance of the horseshoe crab has not changed much in the last 200 million years. It is a reminder that most prehistoric animals were very different from present-day animals.

Max length: 2 cm (¾ in)

worldwide

Hydra

The hydra is a small, simple animal that is related to jellyfish and sea anemones. It lives attached to an underwater surface by a flexible stalk and catches tiny food particles with its tentacles. A hydra can 'walk' slowly across a surface by bending over and performing a slow-motion series of cartwheels with its tentacles.

Ii

Icefish

Found only in the Antarctic Ocean, icefish can withstand temperatures below the freezing point of water thanks to special antifreeze chemicals in their blood. These chemicals affect the blood in other ways, too. Icefish do not have red blood – their blood is colourless.

Max length: 71 cm (28 in)

Iguana

The marine iguana, which is found only on the Galapagos Islands, has a unique lifestyle for a lizard. Although it spends a lot of time on rocks, basking in the sun like other lizards, the marine iguana is equally at home in the sea. It dives a couple of metres below the surface to eat seaweed, which is its main source of food.

Max length: 1.3 m (4¼ ft)

Fact
The marine iguana has a unique way of getting rid of excess salt – it sneezes out salt crystals.

Indri

Max length: 91 cm (36 in)

The indri is the
largest of the lemurs,
which are found only on
the island of Madagascar in
the Indian Ocean. Elsewhere in the world,
lemurs died out long ago and were replaced
by monkeys and apes. Local people call
the indri the 'little father'
of the forest. When it
is on the ground, the
indri moves about with
a series of leaps and jumps.

Max length: 9 mm (½ in)

Moth

Seed

Jumping bean

A real jumping bean is actually the
fallen seed of a Mexican plant that
contains the caterpillar of a small moth
called *Cydia saltitans*. As the caterpillar
develops and moves about inside the seed,
especially when warmed by the sun,
it makes the seed appear to jump about
on the ground.

27

Kk

Max length: 2 m (6½ ft)

Kangaroo

The Australian red kangaroo is the largest of all the marsupials – mammals that carry their young in a pouch. There are many different species of kangaroo. Some are small and live in trees. Those that live on the ground, like the red kangaroo, move about with a unique jumping action, and cannot walk normally like most other mammals.

Fact
The kangaroo rat that lives in the deserts of the southwestern USA is not a marsupial and is only distantly related to true kangaroos.

Kiwi

The kiwi is the national bird of New Zealand, which is the only place that these weird, flightless birds are found. The kiwi has soft, hair-like feathers and no tail. It lives mainly in wooded areas and is rarely seen during the day. At night, it comes out of hiding and uses its long beak to probe for insects and worms in the soil.

Max length: 40 cm (15¾ in)

Koala

Max height: 82 cm (32 in)

Although the koala is often called a bear, it is not a bear at all and is not even a close relative. This Australian mammal is a marsupial that spends almost its entire life in eucalyptus trees where it feeds on the leaves. Unfortunately, the leaves do not provide the koala with very much energy – so it is very slow moving and sleeps for much of each day.

Lamprey

Max length: 51 cm (20 in)

The sea lamprey is an unusual fish that is half parasite and half predator. Unlike nearly all other vertebrates, the lamprey does not have a hinged jaw. Instead, it has a sucker-like mouth with a ring of sharp teeth. The lamprey attaches itself to the sides of bigger fish and starts to eat its way into its victim.

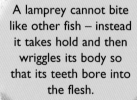

A lamprey cannot bite like other fish – instead it takes hold and then wriggles its body so that its teeth bore into the flesh.

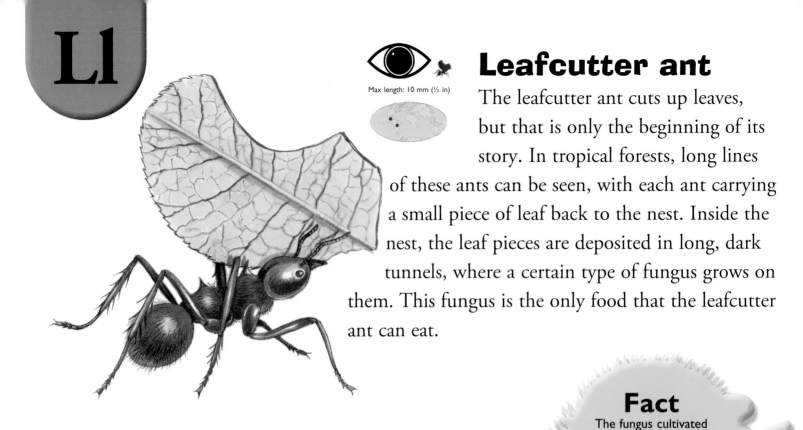

Ll

Leafcutter ant

Max length: 10 mm (½ in)

The leafcutter ant cuts up leaves, but that is only the beginning of its story. In tropical forests, long lines of these ants can be seen, with each ant carrying a small piece of leaf back to the nest. Inside the nest, the leaf pieces are deposited in long, dark tunnels, where a certain type of fungus grows on them. This fungus is the only food that the leafcutter ant can eat.

Fact
The fungus cultivated by leafcutter ants is a unique type that is found only in ant nests.

Leafy sea dragon

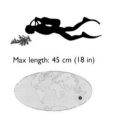

Max length: 45 cm (18 in)

The leafy sea dragon is closely related to the sea horse, and has the same distinctly un-fishlike head. The shape of the rest of the sea dragon's body is difficult to make out because it has so many leaf-like flaps of skin. These 'leaves' provide excellent camouflage when the animal is hiding among coral and seaweed.

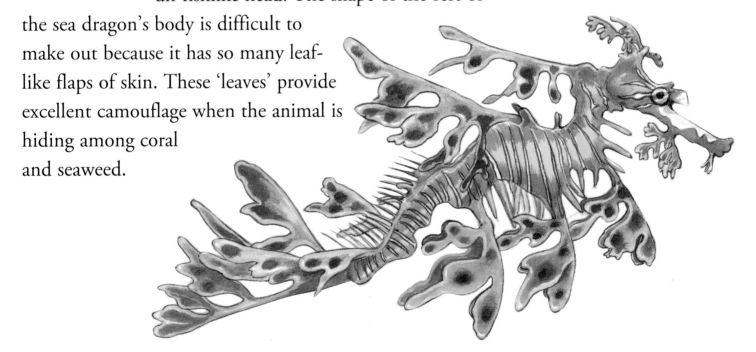

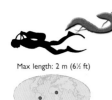

Max length: 2 m (6½ ft)

Lungfish

The lungfish is another of nature's 'living fossils'. Most of its relatives died out millions of years ago. Lungfish live in shallow freshwater streams that are likely to dry up during the summer. Before this happens, the fish burrows into mud and stops using its gills to breathe. Instead, it uses the single lung that gives the fish its name. This lung allows it to breathe air.

Max height: 1.2 m (4 ft)

Macaque

The macaque is often known as the snow monkey, and with good reason. These medium-sized monkeys live in northern Japan in far colder conditions than any of their primate relatives. One trick they have learned for keeping warm is to take advantage of the natural volcanic springs and soak themselves in the hot water.

Mm

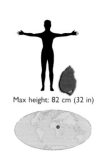

Max height: 82 cm (32 in)

Mandrill

The mandrill is the largest of all mokeys and was once found across much of Africa, but it is now quite rare. It lives in groups (known as troops) of up to 250 individuals, led by the male with the most colourful face markings and the sharpest teeth. The distinctive markings make this monkey stand out amoung others. The front teeth of a fully-grown male mandrill can be more than 6.3 cm (2½ in) long.

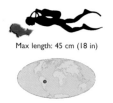

Max length: 45 cm (18 in)

Matamata

This turtle lives in pools and streams in the tropical rainforests of South America. The water is often very muddy and so the matamata cannot rely on eyesight to find its prey. Instead, it waits in ambush just below the surface. The flaps of skin on the sides of its head are not camouflage – the turtle uses them as sense organs to detect the movement of underwater prey.

Max length: 2 cm (¾ in)

worldwide

Mayfly

An adult mayfly has an unusually short life – only about 20–30 hours. During this short time, it has to learn how to fly and find a mate. This is made easier by the fact that all the mayfly larvae (juvenile forms) in a particular area become adult at exactly the same time. On these 'mayfly nights' in spring, the air can be thick with thousands of flying adults.

Fact

Mayflies spend most of their lives as larvae that live in ponds or rivers.

Fact

Mole crickets are usually found near water. They use their short, powerful front legs to dig burrows in damp soil or sand.

Max length: 5 cm (2 in)

worldwide

Mole cricket

Like the mammals they are named after, these weird insects are covered with soft, velvety hairs and live in underground burrows. The mole cricket is also one of the loudest insects. The call of a male in its burrow can be heard at a distance of more than 1.5 km (1 mile).

Mm
Nn

Max length: 25 cm (10 in)

Mudskipper

This small fish lives in coastal mangrove swamps, but is as much at home on land as it is in the water. Twice a day when the tide goes out, the mudskipper prefers to stay where it is rather than go out with the sea. It moves about on mud by using its fins to get a grip on the surface. Some mudskippers even climb up into mangrove trees.

Max length: 20 cm (8 in)

worldwide

Nautilus

The pearly nautilus is another 'living fossil'. Most of its close relatives died out millions of years ago. The nautilus is rarely seen when alive because it lives in deep water, although its shell is often washed up on shore. There are gas-filled chambers inside the shell, which the nautilus uses to control the depth at which it swims.

Fact
The pearly nautilus is strikingly similar to the extinct animals known as ammonites.

Nematode

Max length: 2 mm (1/16 in)

worldwide

The nematode is a microscopically tiny worm that lives in almost every type of soil. Some nematodes are predators while others eat plants. One particular nematode, *Caenorhabditis elegans*, is famous for a very weird reason. Every single worm has exactly the same number of cells in its body – 959, which makes it especially important for scientific research.

Max length: 2.5 cm (1 in)

Net-casting spider

Some spiders spin large webs that stretch across a wide space. The net-casting spider has a different trick. It hangs beneath a branch and spins a small web that it holds between its front legs. When an insect flies within range, the spider throws its net into the air to entangle its unsuspecting prey.

Fact
Net-casting spiders are sometimes called ogre-faced spiders because two of their eyes are much larger than the other six.

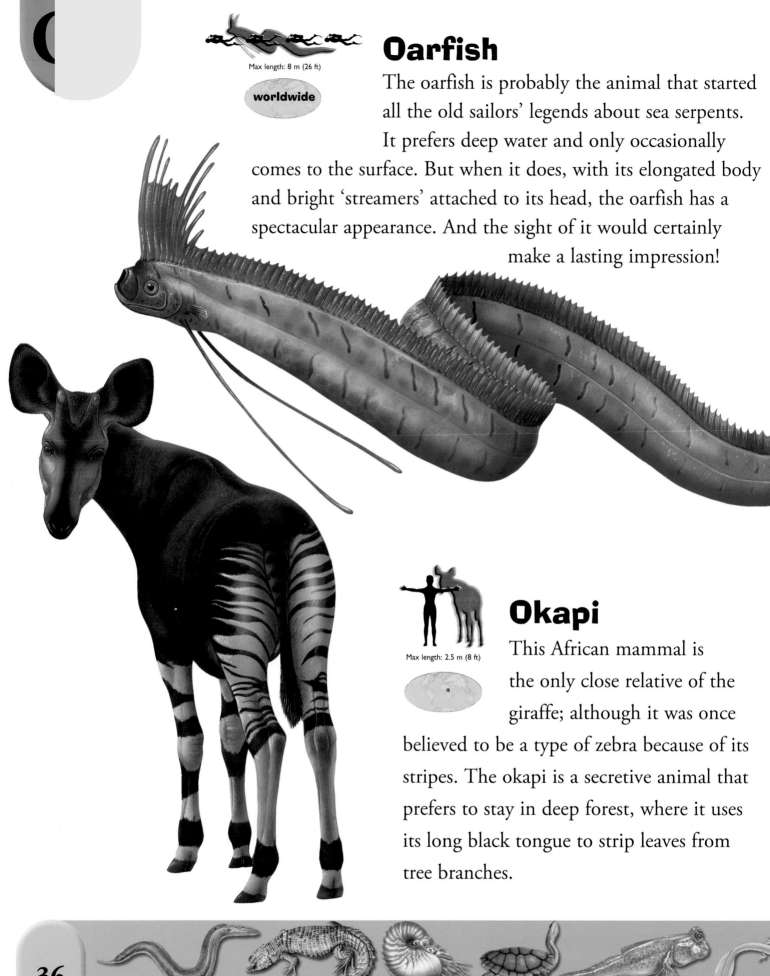

Max length: 8 m (26 ft)

worldwide

Oarfish

The oarfish is probably the animal that started all the old sailors' legends about sea serpents. It prefers deep water and only occasionally comes to the surface. But when it does, with its elongated body and bright 'streamers' attached to its head, the oarfish has a spectacular appearance. And the sight of it would certainly make a lasting impression!

Max length: 2.5 m (8 ft)

Okapi

This African mammal is the only close relative of the giraffe; although it was once believed to be a type of zebra because of its stripes. The okapi is a secretive animal that prefers to stay in deep forest, where it uses its long black tongue to strip leaves from tree branches.

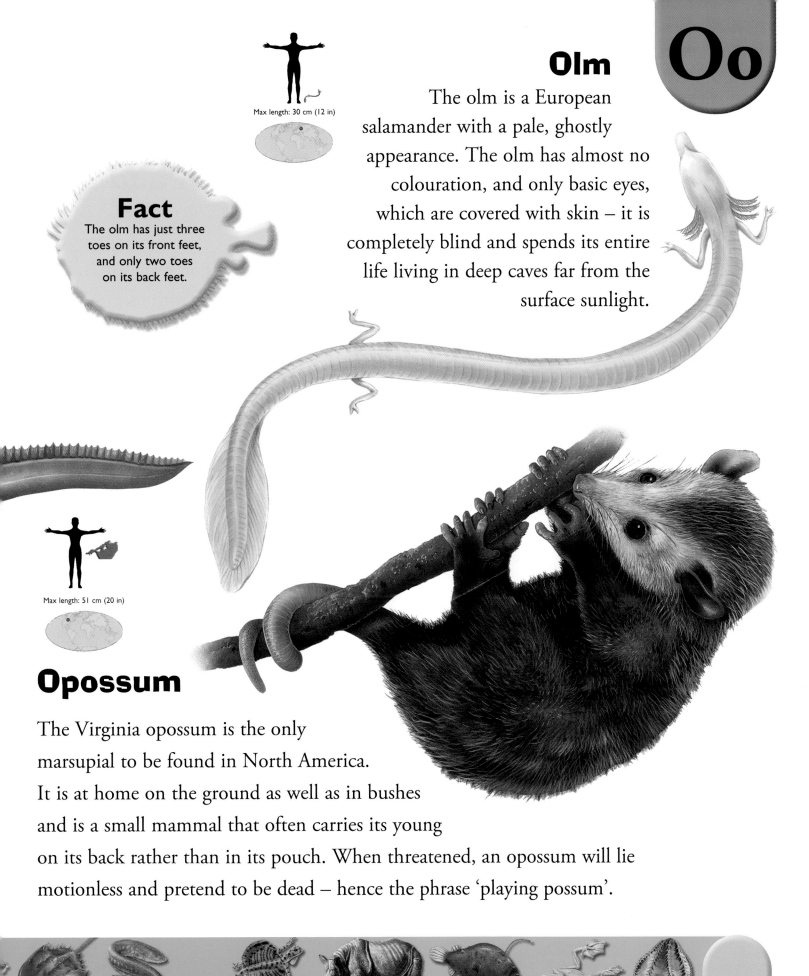

Oo

Olm

The olm is a European salamander with a pale, ghostly appearance. The olm has almost no colouration, and only basic eyes, which are covered with skin – it is completely blind and spends its entire life living in deep caves far from the surface sunlight.

Max length: 30 cm (12 in)

Fact
The olm has just three toes on its front feet, and only two toes on its back feet.

Max length: 51 cm (20 in)

Opossum

The Virginia opossum is the only marsupial to be found in North America. It is at home on the ground as well as in bushes and is a small mammal that often carries its young on its back rather than in its pouch. When threatened, an opossum will lie motionless and pretend to be dead – hence the phrase 'playing possum'.

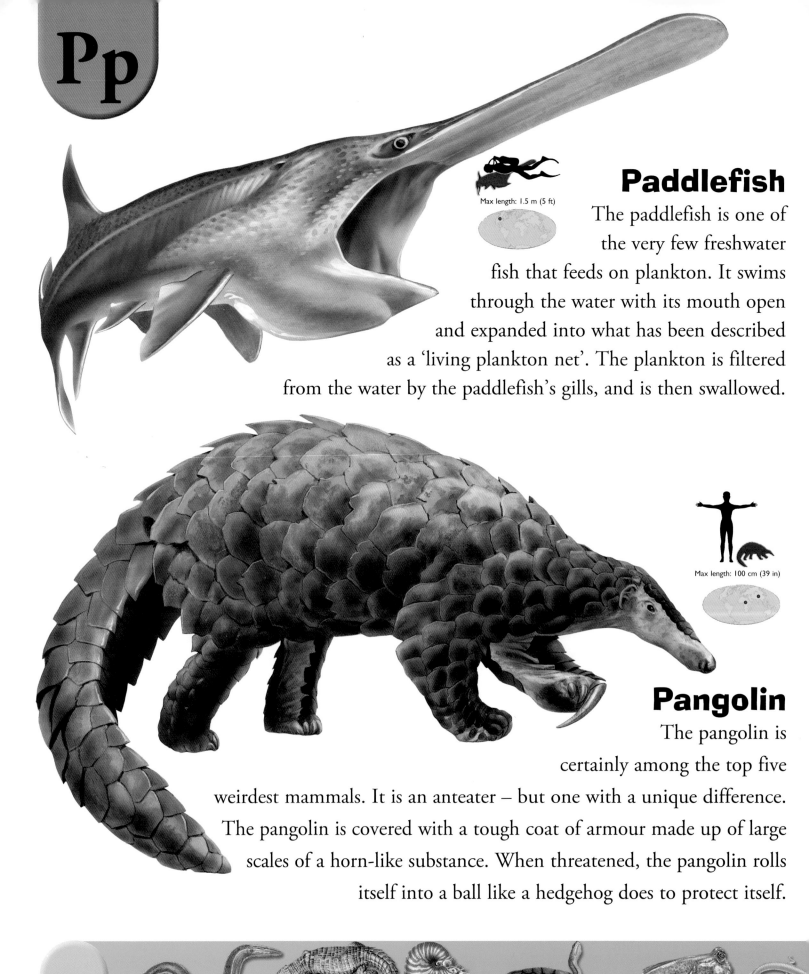

Pp

Paddlefish

Max length: 1.5 m (5 ft)

The paddlefish is one of the very few freshwater fish that feeds on plankton. It swims through the water with its mouth open and expanded into what has been described as a 'living plankton net'. The plankton is filtered from the water by the paddlefish's gills, and is then swallowed.

Max length: 100 cm (39 in)

Pangolin

The pangolin is certainly among the top five weirdest mammals. It is an anteater – but one with a unique difference. The pangolin is covered with a tough coat of armour made up of large scales of a horn-like substance. When threatened, the pangolin rolls itself into a ball like a hedgehog does to protect itself.

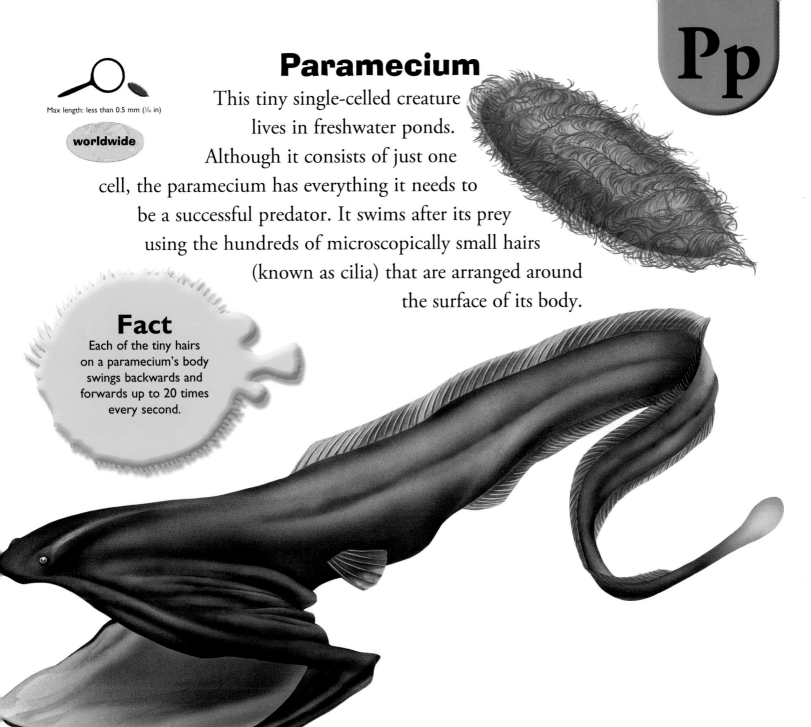

Paramecium

Max length: less than 0.5 mm (⅟₆₄ in)

worldwide

This tiny single-celled creature lives in freshwater ponds. Although it consists of just one cell, the paramecium has everything it needs to be a successful predator. It swims after its prey using the hundreds of microscopically small hairs (known as cilia) that are arranged around the surface of its body.

Fact

Each of the tiny hairs on a paramecium's body swings backwards and forwards up to 20 times every second.

Pelican eel

Max length: 100 cm (39 in)

worldwide

The pelican eel is a weird deep-sea fish that is also known as the gulper eel. It has a slim body and an expandable stomach. By opening its mouth to the widestextent, the pelican eel can swallow other fish that are the same size as itself.

Potto

This small African mammal is related to bush babies and lemurs. Although it is slow moving, the potto is an extremely agile climber. At night it searches tree branches for fruit and insects. To help protect it from predators, the potto has areas of hard skin on its neck and back, which it can use as a shield.

Max length: 40 cm (15¾ in)

Pronghorn

The pronghorn is found only in North America and is another of those animals that is in a class of its own. It is neither a deer nor an antelope, but is classified somewhere between these two groups. The pronghorn is also an extremely fast runner, and can easily outrun a horse.

Max length: 1.5 m (5 ft)

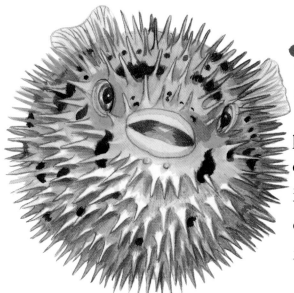

Puffer fish

Max length: 30 cm (1 ft)

When it is quietly going about its business, the puffer fish of the Pacific Ocean looks rather like any other fish. But if you disturb one, the sudden change is quite amazing. The fish puffs itself up into a spine-covered ball that is too large and prickly for most marine predators to swallow.

Pussmoth caterpillar

Max length: 2.5 cm (1 in)

Caterpillars are the soft-bodied larvae (juvenile forms) of moths and butterflies. They are a favourite food of many bird and insect predators. The caterpillar of the pussmoth has a weird form of defence. When threatened, it raises its head, waves its tail and squirts a natural acid at its attacker from a gland in its throat.

Pycnogonid

Max length: 50 cm (19¾ in)

worldwide

Pycnogonid is the scientific name for a sea spider. This weird animal is only distantly related to the land-living and diving spiders that are much more familiar. Sea spiders are predators that feed on soft-bodied animals such as sea anemones. The largest sea spiders are found in cold polar waters. Elsewhere, they rarely reach more than a few centimetres in diameter.

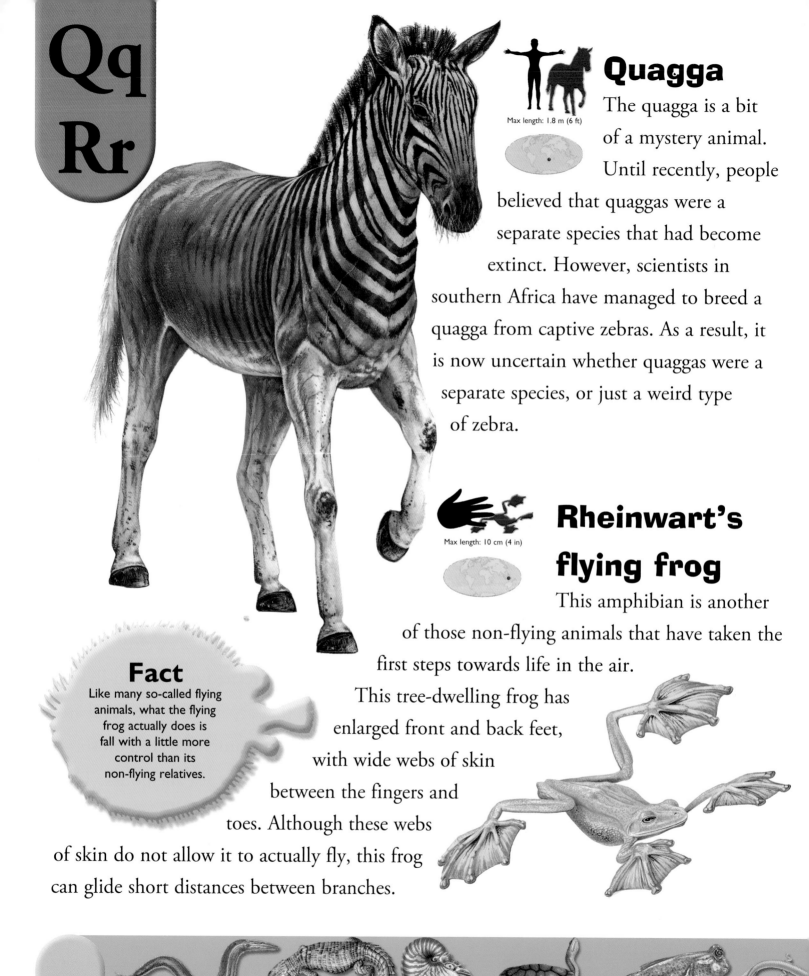

Qq
Rr

Quagga

Max length: 1.8 m (6 ft)

The quagga is a bit of a mystery animal. Until recently, people believed that quaggas were a separate species that had become extinct. However, scientists in southern Africa have managed to breed a quagga from captive zebras. As a result, it is now uncertain whether quaggas were a separate species, or just a weird type of zebra.

Rheinwart's flying frog

Max length: 10 cm (4 in)

This amphibian is another of those non-flying animals that have taken the first steps towards life in the air. This tree-dwelling frog has enlarged front and back feet, with wide webs of skin between the fingers and toes. Although these webs of skin do not allow it to actually fly, this frog can glide short distances between branches.

Fact
Like many so-called flying animals, what the flying frog actually does is fall with a little more control than its non-flying relatives.

Max length: 3.5 m (11½ ft)

Rhinoceros

The Javan rhinoceros, which is critically endangered, has unusually hairless skin for a mammal. Only its ears and the tip of its tail have hairs. This species of rhinoceros is found in Indonesia and has just a single small horn on its snout – some individuals have no horn at all.

Max length: 6.5 cm (2½ in)

Rhinoceros beetle

The rhinoceros beetle is found throughout southern Asia and is one of the largest and strongest of all beetles – it can carry 850 times its own weight! Both males and females have the characteristic 'horn' in front of their eyes, although the male horn is usually larger. Despite its fearsome appearance, this insect does not bite – it feeds on vegetation.

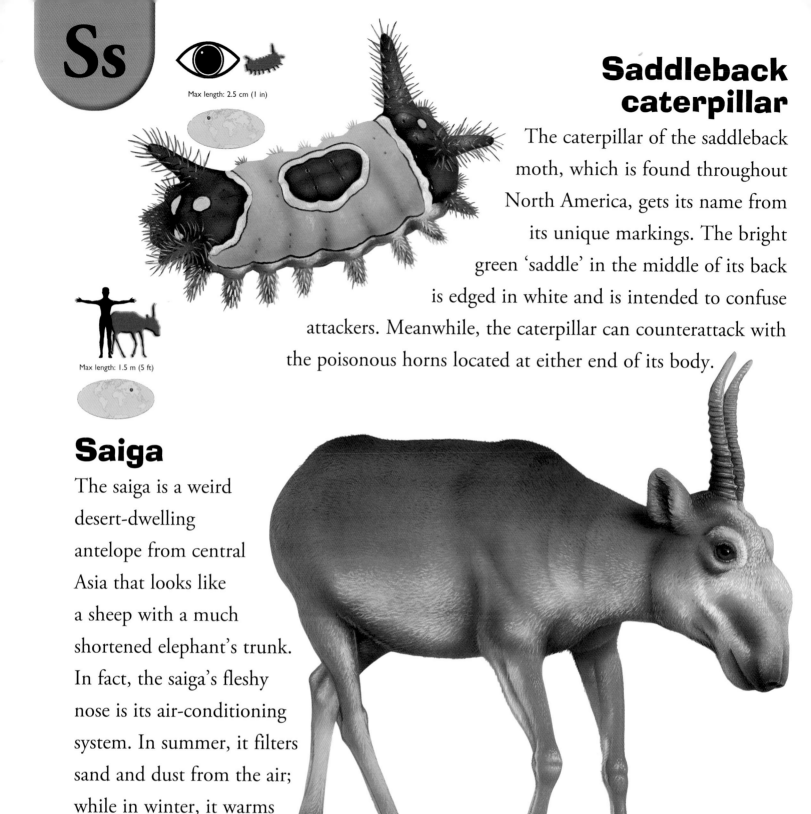

Ss

Max length: 2.5 cm (1 in)

Max length: 1.5 m (5 ft)

Saddleback caterpillar

The caterpillar of the saddleback moth, which is found throughout North America, gets its name from its unique markings. The bright green 'saddle' in the middle of its back is edged in white and is intended to confuse attackers. Meanwhile, the caterpillar can counterattack with the poisonous horns located at either end of its body.

Saiga

The saiga is a weird desert-dwelling antelope from central Asia that looks like a sheep with a much shortened elephant's trunk. In fact, the saiga's fleshy nose is its air-conditioning system. In summer, it filters sand and dust from the air; while in winter, it warms up cold air before the air enters the animal's lungs.

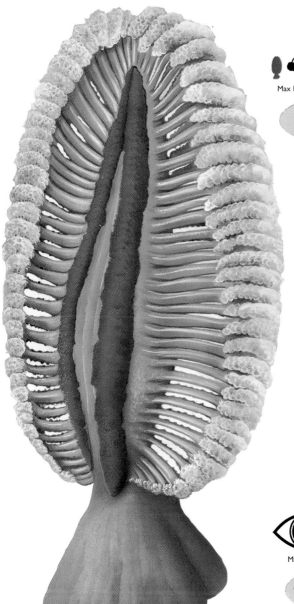

Sea pen

Max length: 45 cm (18 in)

The sea pen got its name because it looks like an old-fashioned quill pen made from a feather. This weird undersea animal is in fact related to reef-forming corals. The sea pen collects plankton from the water. It is known as a soft coral because it does not produce a stony skeleton.

Fact

In ancient times, people believed that sea pens were plants rather than animals.

Max length: 2 m (6½ ft)

worldwide

A slime mould can be a very small and very weird organism often found on the ground in forests. Normally it consists of many thousands of tiny separate amoebas that live, move and feed independently. Sometimes, however, all the amoebas gather and form a small, worm-like blob that wriggles along the forest floor.

Ss

Max length: 25 cm (10 in)

Snake-necked turtle

The snake-necked turtle is found in the rivers of eastern Australia. The head and neck of this unusual reptile are often longer than the rest of its body. The snake-necked turtle shoots out its long neck to snatch passing fish. The long neck also allows the turtle to breathe at the surface of the water while its body remains completely under he water.

Max length: 100 cm (39 in)

worldwide

Fact
Most sponges have a 'skeleton' that is made from minerals extracted from the surrounding water.

Sponge

Until quite recently people believed that sponges were plants rather than animals. In fact, sponges are just about as simple as a multi-celled animal (made up of more than one cell) can be. A sponge has no moving parts. It simply allows water to flow through it and traps tiny food particles. These are then absorbed directly into the sponge's body.

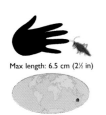

Max length: 6.5 cm (2½ in)

Spotted leaf katydid

The Australian spotted leaf katydid is one of the few insects that makes a disease a part of its disguise. The black spots on the animal's green body look exactly like the leaves of a tree suffering from a plant disease. This disguise attracts fewer predators and helps to keep it safe.

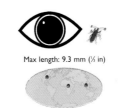

Max length: 9.3 mm (⅓ in)

Stalk-eyed fly

This weird Y-shaped insect has eyes on stalks that are further apart than its overall length. Scientists are unsure why the stalk-eyed fly has such a curious arrangement. The extreme distance between the eyes may help the insect to get a better view of the world. Alternatively, they may be designed just to impress prospective mates.

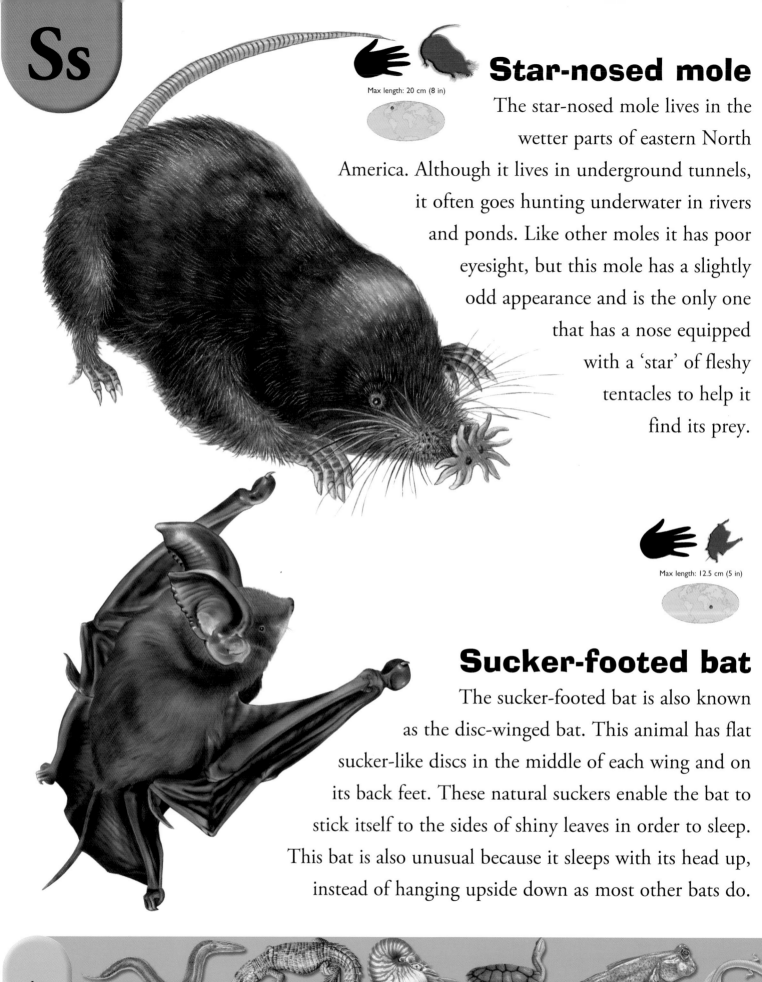

Max length: 20 cm (8 in)

Star-nosed mole

The star-nosed mole lives in the wetter parts of eastern North America. Although it lives in underground tunnels, it often goes hunting underwater in rivers and ponds. Like other moles it has poor eyesight, but this mole has a slightly odd appearance and is the only one that has a nose equipped with a 'star' of fleshy tentacles to help it find its prey.

Max length: 12.5 cm (5 in)

Sucker-footed bat

The sucker-footed bat is also known as the disc-winged bat. This animal has flat sucker-like discs in the middle of each wing and on its back feet. These natural suckers enable the bat to stick itself to the sides of shiny leaves in order to sleep. This bat is also unusual because it sleeps with its head up, instead of hanging upside down as most other bats do.

Max length: 11 cm (4⅓ in)

Tadpole shrimp

This small animal looks a little like a tadpole (juvenile frog or toad) to the unaided eye, but with a magnifier, it is easy to see the curved shield that covers most of the animal's body. The tadpole shrimp is a crustacean and is related to other shrimps and crabs. Unlike most of its relatives, the tadpole shrimp lives in freshwater pools – often in dry regions.

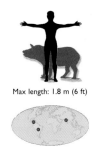

Max length: 1.8 m (6 ft)

Tapir

The mountain tapir is one of just four species of tapir. This weird, forest-dwelling mammal is a plant eater and has a short trunk that it uses to strip leaves from branches. Three tapir species, including the mountain tapir, live in Central and South America, while the fourth is found many thousands of kilometres away in southern Asia.

Fact
The mountain tapir is the most furry of the tapirs because it lives in cooler conditions than its relatives, which are tropical forest animals.

Tt

Tear moth

Max length: 8 cm (3 in)

The tear moth has very unusual feeding habits – it does not eat meat and does not eat vegetation. Instead, this small moth obtains all the nourishment it needs by drinking the tears of large mammals. One particular species will even feed from the eyes of human beings, although they generally feed on animals such as water buffaloes.

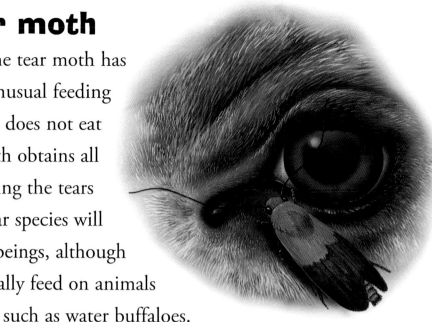

Tentacled snake

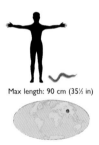

Max length: 90 cm (35½ in)

The tentacled snake is a weird reptile that is found only in certain parts of Asia. It lives in and around rivers and can stay underwater for at least five minutes, before surfacing to breathe. Scientists believe that the weird tentacles on its snout, which are unique to this snake, are used to find prey such as frogs and fish along muddy river bottoms.

Three-toed sloth

The South American three-toed sloth is the
only mammal that does not normally hold
its head higher than its feet. This tree-dwelling animal
spends almost its whole life hanging upside down from
tree branches. As a result, the organs inside its body
are in different locations compared with the normal
mammal arrangement.

Max length: 58 cm (23 in)

Toucan

This bird from the tropical forests of South
America has an enormous orange beak that is much
bigger than its head. The extremely long beak can reach fruit on nearby
branches that are too thin to take the bird's weight. The toucan first
grabs a fruit with the tip of its beak and then throws it into the air to
be caught and swallowed.

Max length: 63 cm (25 in)

Tt

Max length: 35 cm (13¾ in)

Triclad flatworm

The flatworm is not divided into segments like earthworms. It is mostly a small animal that lives in water. Some flatworms, however, have taken to life on land and these are some of the largest and strangest looking. The brightly coloured species *Bipalium kewense*, from Hawaii, makes a striking sight as it slithers through a forest.

Fact

The flatworm Bipalium kewense has been spread around the world through the trade in tropical plants and is now well established in California.

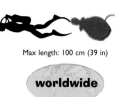

Max length: 100 cm (39 in)

worldwide

Triplewart seadevil

The triplewart seadevil is a deep-sea anglerfish. The female attracts prey with bait that sends out light and dangles in front of its huge mouth. What is weird about it is that the male is tiny in comparison to the female. It lives as a parasite, permanently attached to the body of a female seadevil.

Max length: 80 cm (31½ in)

Tuatara

The tuatara looks very similar to most lizards, but it is in fact quite a different sort of animal. The two species of tuatara are the only survivors of a prehistoric group of reptiles – all the other members of the group died out more than 100 million years ago. Today, the tuatara is found only on small, isolated islands near New Zealand.

Max length: 55 cm (21¾ in)

Tube-nosed fruit bat

Most bats have strangely shaped noses because they use echolocation, where sound waves are used to locate prey, but the tube-nosed fruit bat from the Philippines just has a good sense of smell. The fruit bat feeds on nectar and fruit and has elongated nostrils, which act like direction finders, helping the animal to locate the scent of flowers and ripe fruit.

Upside-down catfish

Max length: 10 cm (4 in)

This African fish lives up to its name. Most catfish are known as bottom-feeders because they feed near the bed of rivers and lakes. The upside-down catfish swims upside down at the surface, in order to feed on tiny animals clinging to the underside of rocks and floating vegetation.

Max length: 9 cm (3½ in)

Vampire bat

The vampire bat lives in parts of South America and feeds on blood, although it does not suck the blood into its mouth. It bites its victims, and then laps up the blood with its tongue. Contrary to popular belief, vampire bats do not often swoop down and bite their victims' necks. These bats are more likely to approach their prey by hopping along the ground, and biting the victim on the leg.

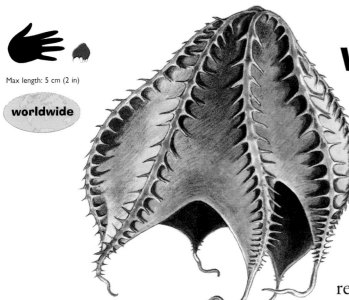

Max length: 5 cm (2 in)

worldwide

Vampire Squid

This small deep-sea mollusc has eight swimming tentacles, which are linked by webs of skin. It also has two additional feeding tentacles for grabbing prey. When threatened, the vampire squid enfolds itself in its webbed tentacles, revealing sharp spines underneath.

Max length: 3.8 cm (1½ in)

worldwide

Velvet worm

The velvet worm is a strange animal that lives on forest floors in warm areas. It looks rather like a giant caterpillar, but is in fact in a class of its own. The velvet worm combines some of the characteristics of two other animal groups – the true worms (such as the earthworm) and arthropods (insects and crustaceans for example).

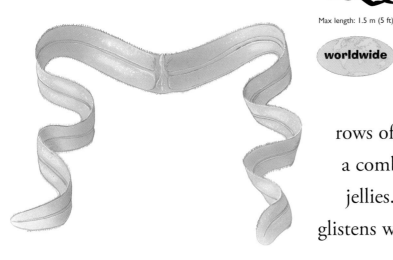

Max length: 1.5 m (5 ft)

worldwide

Venus's girdle

This strange sea creature belongs to a group of animals known as comb jellies. It has a soft body covered with rows of tiny projections that look like the teeth of a comb. Venus's girdle is one of the largest comb jellies. It has a completely transparent body that glistens with a blue-green iridescence in sunlight. At night, the girdle emits a soft green glow.

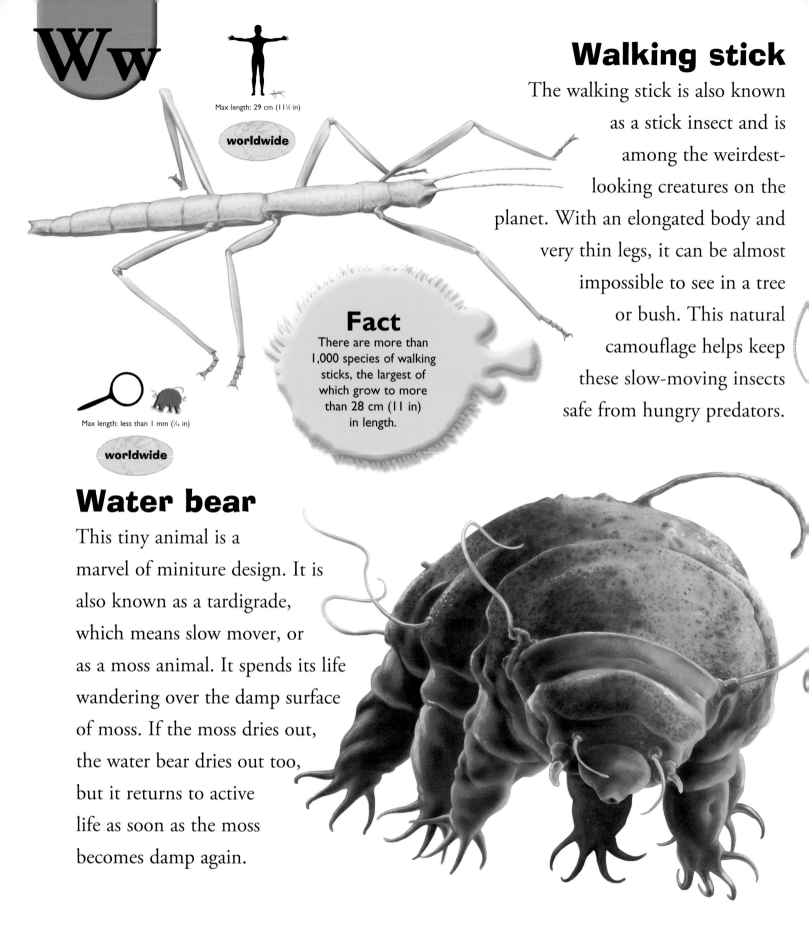

Ww

Max length: 29 cm (11½ in)

worldwide

Walking stick

The walking stick is also known as a stick insect and is among the weirdest-looking creatures on the planet. With an elongated body and very thin legs, it can be almost impossible to see in a tree or bush. This natural camouflage helps keep these slow-moving insects safe from hungry predators.

Fact
There are more than 1,000 species of walking sticks, the largest of which grow to more than 28 cm (11 in) in length.

Max length: less than 1 mm (¹⁄₁₆ in)

worldwide

Water bear

This tiny animal is a marvel of miniture design. It is also known as a tardigrade, which means slow mover, or as a moss animal. It spends its life wandering over the damp surface of moss. If the moss dries out, the water bear dries out too, but it returns to active life as soon as the moss becomes damp again.

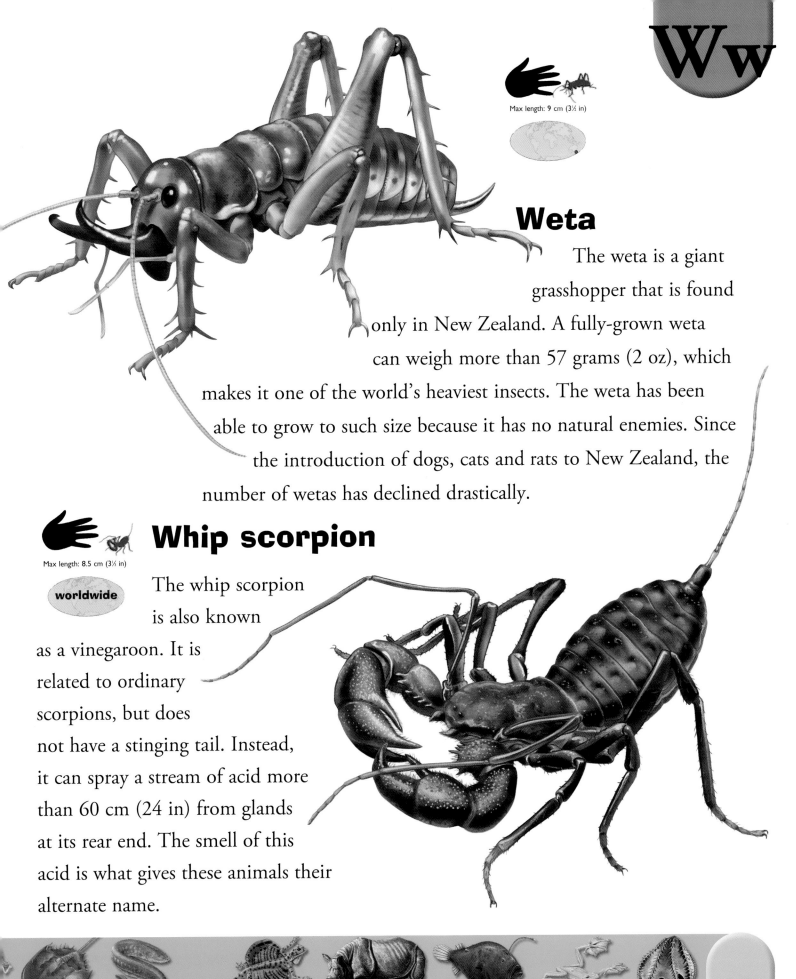

Max length: 9 cm (3½ in)

Weta

The weta is a giant grasshopper that is found only in New Zealand. A fully-grown weta can weigh more than 57 grams (2 oz), which makes it one of the world's heaviest insects. The weta has been able to grow to such size because it has no natural enemies. Since the introduction of dogs, cats and rats to New Zealand, the number of wetas has declined drastically.

Max length: 8.5 cm (3⅓ in)

worldwide

Whip scorpion

The whip scorpion is also known as a vinegaroon. It is related to ordinary scorpions, but does not have a stinging tail. Instead, it can spray a stream of acid more than 60 cm (24 in) from glands at its rear end. The smell of this acid is what gives these animals their alternate name.

Ww
Xx

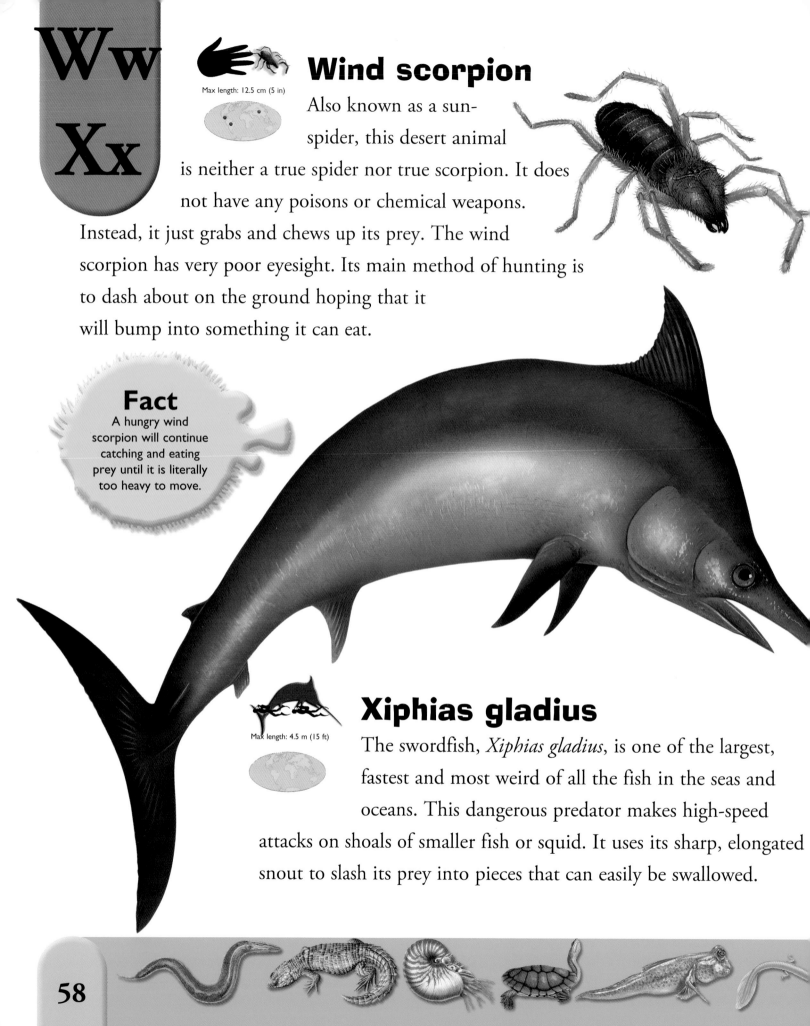

Wind scorpion

Max length: 12.5 cm (5 in)

Also known as a sun-spider, this desert animal is neither a true spider nor true scorpion. It does not have any poisons or chemical weapons. Instead, it just grabs and chews up its prey. The wind scorpion has very poor eyesight. Its main method of hunting is to dash about on the ground hoping that it will bump into something it can eat.

Fact
A hungry wind scorpion will continue catching and eating prey until it is literally too heavy to move.

Xiphias gladius

Max length: 4.5 m (15 ft)

The swordfish, *Xiphias gladius*, is one of the largest, fastest and most weird of all the fish in the seas and oceans. This dangerous predator makes high-speed attacks on shoals of smaller fish or squid. It uses its sharp, elongated snout to slash its prey into pieces that can easily be swallowed.

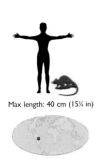

Max length: 40 cm (15¼ in)

Yapok

This South American mammal is the only marsupial (out of more than 290 species) that lives in water.

It has webbed toes on its back legs for better swimming and a watertight pouch to keep its young safe and dry. The yapok feeds on fish and frogs that it grabs with its front feet, which are completely clawless.

Max length: 33 cm (13 in)

Zimbabwe girdled lizard

This weird African lizard has a flattened body and a tail covered with sharp spines. If it senses danger, the lizard squeezes its body into a crack in a rock or under a stone. It then uses its tail to block the crack so that any attacker gets a face full of spines.

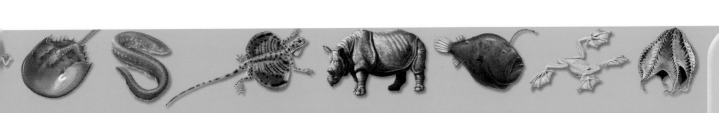

Glossary

Amphibian An air-breathing animal with a backbone that lays its eggs in water. Frogs and toads are the most commonly encountered types of amphibian.

Bat One of about 1,000 species of flying mammals that are mainly active only at night.

Bird A warm-blooded animal that has a body covered with feathers and that lays hard-shelled eggs.

Camouflage Shape, colour and pattern that help an animal blend in with its background so that it is hard to see.

Carnivorous Describes a meat-eating animal.

Caterpillar The larva (juvenile form) of a moth or butterfly.

Cold-blooded Describes any animal that relies on the environment to maintain its body temperature. Reptiles, amphibians and fish are the main groups of cold-blooded animals, along with insects, spiders, molluscs and all other animals without backbones.

Corrosive Describes a substance that can damage living tissue and other materials.

Crustacean Type of multi-legged animal that is found almost exclusively in the sea. Crabs, shrimps and lobsters are all crustaceans.

Domesticated Describes a species that was once wild, but which has become a separate species after many hundreds of years of being a farm animal or pet.

Echolocation Method of detecting prey and obstacles by means of sound waves that is used by many bats and some sea mammals.

Eel One of a group of unusual fish that have long, slender, scale-less bodies, and which have either very small fins or none at all.

Endangered Describes a species that exists in such small numbers that it is in danger of dying out completely.

Glossary

Extinct Describes a species that no longer exists.

Fin A body part which projects from the back, sides or underside of a fish.

Fish A water-living animal that has a body covered with scales, and which breathes through gills.

Freshwater
Rainwater, river water and the water in most lakes, is called freshwater because it contains no salt.

Fungi A form of life that is neither plant nor animal. Fungus grows mainly underground. Mushrooms are the most common type of fungus.

Gills The organs which fish, and some other water animals, use to breathe underwater. In most fish, the gills are visible as one or more slits on the sides of the head.

Gland A body part that produces substances that are used elsewhere.

Insect Small, six-legged animal that does not have a backbone and which often has wings.

Larva (plural larvae)
The juvenile or young form of an insect that changes its appearance when it becomes an adult.

Living fossil A species that has survived for millions of years after similar species became extinct.

Glossary

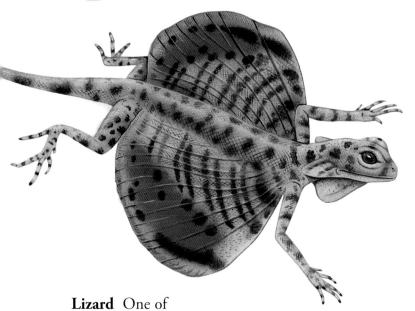

Lizard One of a large group of generally small- to medium-sized, land-living reptiles.

Mammal A warm-blooded animal with a backbone that produces live-born young. Most mammals are covered with hair and live on land. There are a few marine mammals such as seals and whales.

Mangrove A tree that can survive with its roots immersed in water, and which grows along many tropical coastlines.

Marsupial One of a group of mammals that carry and care for their young in a special pouch on the female body.

Mollusc One of a group of soft-bodied animals. Some molluscs, for example snails, make hard, protective shells for themselves. Another group of molluscs, that includes octopus and squid, have no external shell, and are equipped with long, grasping tentacles.

Oxygen The chemical gas in air, which is essential for living things. Land animals take in oxygen directly from the air. Fish and most other sea creatures extract oxygen that is dissolved in water.

Parasite An animal that lives in or on the body of another animal (called the host) and which feeds on the host.

Plankton Tiny plants and animals that float in water and provide food for many of the larger water animals.

Poison Any substance that is harmful to living things.

Predator An animal that hunts and eats other animals.

Prey An animal that is hunted and eaten by others.

Primate One of a group of mainly tree-dwelling animals that have the same basic body plan as human beings.

Glossary

Species The particular scientific group to which an individual animal (or plant) belongs. Each species is a unique design and has a two-part scientific name. Members of the same species all share the same characteristics and differ only slightly in colour or size.

Reptile A cold-blooded animal with a backbone that breathes air and produces live young or shelled eggs. Crocodiles, lizards, turtles, tortoises and snakes are all reptiles.

Rodent One of a group of small mammals that includes rats, mice and squirrels, but not rabbits and hares.

Skeleton A structure made of hard substances that supports the body of an animal. The skeleton can be either internal (and arranged around a backbone) as with mammals, birds, reptiles, amphibians and fish, or it can be external as with many other animals such as insects and starfish.

Snake One of a large group of legless reptiles.

Tentacles The long, boneless limbs of some creatures. Tentacles are used for catching prey and are sometimes equipped with stings.

Warm-blooded Describes mammals and birds, which are the only animals that produce their own individual body heat.

Index